OVERTURNED CUPS

Overturned Cups
Lianne M. Bernardo

First Printing: 2021

ISBN: 978-1-7750431-4-0

Note about the font: The font featured in the titles on both the book cover and first page is based on my own penmanship (when writing in print).

An ode to the years
confronted by overturned cups—
But I'm still here.

And though life be hard
as stone and flint and snow
I follow the hymn of water.

"Let the dead bury their dead" they say—
I now know where your dead lie
buried in your chest
as the whole world passes by.
But you do not know it
though you are complicit;
the truth will reveal itself one day
(too late).

The continuum of hurt continues;
who knew this barrel could run so deep?
The past is a distant country
that cannot be emigrated to
and the future is a lonely planet.
The cycle should end, even
as history runs repeatedly
lest the cup of pain overflows,
spills on fertile ground.

And this is where old dreams go to die:
not in evergreen pastures in far off lands,
nor in the flames of high drama and passion
but in the dead of night,
the slow crawl into oblivion,
without a whimper or mourning cry
but in the silence of defeat,
remaining hopes long gone.

I'm tired of the weight
pulling me down,
opening a sink hole
in the middle of nowhere.
I'm tired of this burden
dragging me to the precipice
of the never-ending cyclone
threatening to consume all.
I'm tired of it all,
every stone along the road;
I've forgotten myself
with every stumble and fall.

Take me back to a time
before I knew you
before I knew the possibility of what
    could be.

Will it always be
that I am chasing
ephemerals in the dark,
phantoms in the frost,
illusions in the dark?
There's a tragedy in
these missed connections
and what-ifs lost
to the last rays of the indigo sun.

I will leave my name
in every corner
and every space
we have traversed
so you may not forget me
long after I am gone.

Lo, how this body has suddenly become
a playground under scrutiny
of desire, of survival, of debate.
Questions are brought forth
of the arms and the hips,
the flab of the belly, hair here and there,
a nebula of perplexity, if it were.

The moon is out,
half-bowl of silver
accompanied by a thin spectrum of
    wayward stars.

I wonder what their audience
will bring (me).

There is no hiding from fury,
the molten wave of anger
that overwhelms the heart
and seizes the chest,
changing calm seas to rough waters.

And when it subsides it leaves
a barren wasteland
devoid of trees and birds chirping,
only stony faces and hardened hearts
   beyond repair.

These dreams—
they convalesce between
sleeping and waking,
invisible lines that are
no longer seen as passageways
but merely some wayward thought.

They shall not be coming home,
the youth of the night;
soft beds shall lie cold,
cold and empty bodies lie in slabs.
All the while those invisible hands
sleep well in feathered beds
paid by the bullet,
paid by their blood.

(n.d.)

I hold my heart against my soul,
afraid for anyone to see.
My chest is a shield
made of thorns
that will let no one in.

I took the plunge only
to find myself
in the middle of nowhere
with not a patch of land in sight.
The clouds in the sky are the same—
I've lost my way.

Burn me with gladness
doused in the choice of midnight sadness.
A walk in the dark so empty,
a void so wanting it cannot be free,
 cloying,
 inviting,
a segue into madness.

The dying of the light
bears with it all the hopes of the day.
But the darkness of night
carries its own dreams,
strange magic unseen.

What does it mean
to bleed an ocean
and search for meaning
in a copper-filled sky?
To sink your teeth in fire
lest the emptiness spills
from the cavern where your
    heart used to lie
—thus the ambiguity,
the uncertainty.

Like faint wisp-o-willows
  they fade away,
these precious little dreams
locked so close to the chest.
They were stolen away,
snatched away by unseen villains
    into the dark.
Hollow outlines remain where
    once they lay
standing proudly by the window
draped in moonlight and starlight.
Now the door opens without a stop,
emptiness greets me instead.

The merits of the silent dead
ought to echo for all eternity
over the evils of the few;
the dead gone too soon,
unbeknownst of their fate,
festive grounds soaked in innocent horror.
May the dead's deeds live on,
small comfort to violent chaos,
ripples wide and near but ever going.

(01 October 2017)

Gently but with purpose
I shake these pins
that fasten me down.
Their weight is no longer my concern,
I feel nothing but the breeze.

My roots lie not in the
    history that makes up my blood
    or some distant place my parents
    and grandparents call home
but what lies beneath my feet,
the places around me that I call home.
Saturated in history I am but
my roots do not stir my breast,
my eyes do not cast eastward;
the mind only recalls bleached blocks, shelters
    of the departed,
and unfamiliar faces averse by my presence.
No, my roots do not trigger
    any longing, no curiosity,
    only a shadow of obscure memory.
My roots are here, now.
I am who I am.

Thank you for teaching me
that even friendships have expiry dates,
that forever is subject to change,
that roads can diverge irreparably.

Pain crinkles like dead stars
amassed in one corner of the night sky;
they crumble and they fall,
celestial ash, unwanted.

Sorrow has a compass:
it points to the grave of what
    once was.

You've become your own devils,
  selling your souls for
    power that does not last,
cowering behind forces that
    will not save us but
    bury us into an oblivion
    so deep and so dark
    all will be lost,
    all will be forgotten,
    greatness scorned as some
    dreams that cannot be held.

Welcome to hell.

What is the point of dreams
if they do not come true?

(—*a moment of despair*)

Points of light
faint against an inky sea of night.
Where hope reigns, I know not;
the darkness is all I see.

The moss of the trees,
the burden of existence.

These old stones
cannot contain
my longing for the unknown,
ancient beams of a bygone world,
bearing up the sky of back then.

At the edge of the world
you will find yourself once more.

Maybe this who I am all along:
wind and water,
the coming and going of rain.

Fear is a noose
that tightens its coil
with every thought.
Fear is a trap
waiting in the dark, invisible,
for unsuspecting travellers to fall.

They are riddling my home with bullets,
masking these streets with sorrow.
Hindsight is no solvent replacement
to the empty seats and beds left behind.

(22 July 2018)

Unbox this confusion
with a fury of fireflies
to illuminate the night
and a path forward.
Unburdening the soul is a risk;
    the weight of our sorrows
    a familiar comfort.

Since when have I
transformed into a fury?
Words sharpened at the edges,
up front for the world to see.
Since when have I
raised my head, stood my ground,
      Raised my voice?
When disappointment, betrayal,
      and lack of respect rained down,
An endless storm hammering even
      the firmest of resolves,
      the patience of wise men.
No sheep remain: only lions.

These dreams are little terrors,
miniscule impossibilities
that are difficult to ignore.
But they run red—alive
   against the skin.
Let us take the sledgehammer
   and put it to the test:.
will it shatter like a glass house
    against the sea coast
or crystalise into something finer?

The flower bloomed unexpectedly overnight,
its scent intoxicating,
its petals threatening to fall at any moment.
Its existence is a mystery,
delicate against the coming dawn,
fragile to the passage of time.
Who knows if it will live to see a day whole...

Ice chips form
where summer once bloomed;
the frost is coming,
it's time to say farewell to long sunshine days.

With youth comes recklessness;
with youth comes fear.

She walks into the silence
eyes open and a heart
outfitted with chainmail
to keep intruders out.

I know now
that to love is to dare,
to take a chance,
to take flight.

I know now
that to love is to take a risk,
to surrender,
to let go.

This pump squeezes
that which keeps the blood going
of which we keep going—
But it bounds and it cools
as the agony and uncertainty rises and falls
to that which the human eye
    cannot ascertain.
Abide in me, and set the matter straight
so that this organ can determine life or death
    from this point on.

Hope fades
as the moon passes on to darkness;
no pale light to shine on hidden walkways.
Dreams crash as waves meet the jagged shores
splintered into fractured molecules beyond recall.
Expectations fall through
like wind over sandy dunes
clipping away the mounds,
cutting them off at the knees.

Such desolation awaits
like that of a Russian tragedy—
Life goes on amidst bare trees and muddied waters
snow turned brown by the slush.
And where does the pale life lie but yonder—
beyond the horizon,
across the globe,
greener pastures indeed.

Polite smiles and small conversation
hide the havoc left by chance
by bravery made manifest
now in retrospect inopportune.
Hearty laughter and helping hands
mask the breaking heart
that is crumbling inside translucent walls.
The muscles weaken, the soul is tired,
—defeat has settled in.

Rip at the sinews,
break the bones
for something deeper
lying in wake.

You're a ninja thief,
don't you know?
You've stolen my heart
from behind my rib cage
without me knowing.
And I find you've also
taken my words,
without you realizing,
pretty little things
to string a bracelet by.

How great hope blooms
against so few words
when despair in equal doses
send dreams crashing down
hard.

Love—or something like it—
has made me foolish,
has prompted me out of character,
has made me do things
I've never done out of sense.

Love—or something like it—
has set me in a daze,
has filled my hopes with lofty dreams,
has left me hanging on a wire.

What is life
after knowing you?
Life, the passage of time,
the coming and going of seasons
—but no crinkled smile, no you.

The darkness has won—
there is no parley with the night sky,
no negotiation, no accommodation,
only the conquering.

My thoughts are devoid of you,
but they're empty of everything else too.

Fury—
the fury in the heartbreak,
from those who failed us
and left us behind.

And when will it end,
the splitting the shards
of this broken heart
into a deadly pit of spikes
to which I throw myself on?

I find myself still drawn by your gravity
long after the rainbow bridge has faded...

We are fine, you and I,
save for the emptiness in my chest
where dreams of you and I
once thrived.

I fell for a man with a broken heart.
Silly me: of course his brokenness
would break my heart too.

It cannot be helped:
your nearness still trills my heart,
comforting, close.

But silence cannot be ignored,
the past still looms,
a thorn in the heart.

Your name remains a fixture on my lips
long after hope has faded.

This one-sided romance,
this chemical dream,
is a kind of death,
is a wasteland to hope.

I think I have a stowaway
in my heart...

Who switched on the light
behind your eyes?
They glow like warm caramel,
they startle and surprise.

He could not fall in love
the way a man ought to:
his heart was too broken,
too scared to open up again.

Doubt plagues
where feelings ought to roam
to their natural goals and ends.
But doubt is a ninja,
swift in its discourse,
silent in its judgement—
these feelings stand no chance.

Sadness is a silent sea
invisible to the naked eye,
to distracted society.
It ebbs and it throbs
it rises up, it consumes,
flooding the lungs,
swallowing me whole.

I am the sea,
I am sadness.

The vast emptiness
present in my heart—
who knew all this space
could hurt so much?

Fury unleashed;
can't stop the tides
from swelling against
grainy shores
try as one might—

Water flows.

Golden half-lid in the sky
gazing, searching, listless,
an eye open at night...

Whose soul do you seek,
yellow-eyed, silver-haloed?

There are highs,
there are lows,
there are no mores

(New Year's Day)

You gift me with a smile
even though you're a million heartbeats away.

I am a theatre of wonder,
a cause for daily celebration.

You're still with me
but already I'm living with
only memories
of perfect summer days
smiling together.

Weighing my words
syllable by syllable,
ounce by ounce;
this is how you kill anger.

Organising my feelings
brick by brick,
wading against mud,
the slog of time—
this is how you forgive yourself.

Exile child
you go your own way:
follow the waterways
whatever will bring you to the sea.

Perhaps in the end
we are all paper scraps
   torn apart,
   cast aside,
   beleaguered that our rise and fall
   came and went too soon.

Setting fire to all the mementos
and memories I once loved
for they've all grown legs
and wandered far without me,
without so much as a parting wave of farewell,
left me here confused,
abandoned to memory.

So who gives a damn about
bridges and of letting things go
in the hopes they return:
it's all kindling in the end.

One day I'll wake up
and the pain will be gone
and all memory of you
will be as that of a former wound
I've recovered from.

Friends, like lovers,
ought to come with warning signs:
—they do not complete you
—they do not determine your self-worth
—they can break you apart

(And when they leave
they will track mud
deep into the foundations
of your house)

The weight of fire
shall not be consumed
by an ever abundance of joy
but by the static of flat air,
the dead silence,
the desolation of failed stewardship.

I hold my breath
waiting for you,
a slice of mystery between us
still as dawn.

Somewhere a bird stirs.

Somewhere the sun wakes.

You burn,
the blaze ripping your insides
shattering your limbs,
your lungs, your crown.

I mourn.

(15 April 2019)

The holes in your mind
seems less defined
when the wind blows,
the ground quakes,
the skies sigh.

Your silence screams
into the chambers of my heart
where blood ought to be.
Paper messages flutter
against a stillborn wind,
final destination: unknown.

I search for you in the silence,
I seek you with sleepy wonder.

My stowaway has gone beyond the sea
and I find it is I
without the anchor, not he.

Sadness envelopes
where our words once held weight.

(—*this too shall pass*)

I fear the words are
running out;
I reach inside and
am met with silence.

I once kept the peace
but no more.

I am naked fury.

Tired of playing nice,
tired of being chosen last,
tired of waiting,
tired of excuses,
tired of you.

This is new
as you are new:
no rock left unturned,
no river we dare not cross.

This time my mouth is
not some basket of marbles
held up by rigid ionic columns
begging for a favour.
This time my fingers lay
not waiting for a message
that will never come.
This time my flesh and blood
and soul flares
without reservation.

And just like that I realized
the past is dead and no more:
these words I could never share with you,
these feelings I could never decipher.
I am not who I was before.

I'm in too deep once more
that the only thing to do
is breathe deep and
take the plunge.

(—*maybe it'll be worth it*)

Let's be brave one more time
little heart, and slide our
small, beaten hands
on the steering wheel.

This suit of armour won't shed,
its metal glued directly to my skin;
even if I wanted to, it will not budge.

Help me pry it off.

You've already taken up residency
in my mind,
a stakeholder to my heart
it seems.

My skin is armour
—hardened, rusted, impenetrable.
My skin longs to be human
but it does not know how.

The sun was shining
and the lake was still
but amidst all this
I'm sorry I forgot to
hold your hand.

This mask, I don't know
how much longer I can bear it;
it's cracked and faded
and all that is true
is pouring forth.

Encase this chest
with ice and armour
but still my heart
is bursting
at the seams.

What is the heart
but a punching bag
left out in the open
with no shield?

Let me stare out into oblivion
and feel the wreckage that is my soul.

The silence lengthens,
strains, echoes,
and yet I still yearn
    for your soul
      its quiet radiance,
      its contained chaos.

          (*—it's not over yet*)

To go from souls in sync
to complete disarray—
what a neurotic disaster it was.

Tell me where old dreams
go to die.

Let me tell you about
curvatures and ligaments,
tendons and heartbeats,
breath and bone
and everything that makes us human.

I keep walking in hopes
of finding myself;
she keeps wandering off-course,
lost in the thick brambles and
wildlands somewhere.

When I find her she's in pieces,
lost in thought,
scattered amongst the lava fields.

One minute there's laughter
and the next moment: tears.

A heart so dead
it does not recognize
love when it comes to stay.

(—a fear)

Laughter and calmness:
that is how I'll remember you.

And sometimes in
the depths of night,
amidst the silence,
I remember how it once was
and how it hurt so much afterward.

Slowly but surely
I begin to feel
like myself again;
you're but a distant memory now,
I feel strong again.

I wish you well
but I don't wish you back;
so much has changed,
I've learned to live without your presence.

When faced with our own mortality
we become alone,
petrified organisms
without their claws.

(01 December 2019)

I know now
I am bravery
and madness.

ABOUT THE AUTHOR

Lianne M. Bernardo is from Canada. She has previously written for high school and university publications, online e-zines, and Youth Speak News at the Catholic Register whilst accumulating a stack of unpublished content ranging from novel-length stories to poetry.

You can follow her on Instagram at *@shallibeapoetinstead*

ALSO BY THE AUTHOR

Shall I Be a Poet Instead?

Of Frost and Fury: Poems Written in the Land of Volcanoes and Giants

With Quiet Ardency

Scattered Stars

www.ingramcontent.com/pod-product-compliance
Lightning Source LLC
Chambersburg PA
CBHW032138040426
42449CB00005B/307